Ourselves and other Animals

Contents

Revision

Did you know . . . ?

 There are different kinds of animals but they have things in common.

 Animals need certain things to stay alive and to grow.

Task 1 Similarities and differences between animals

....

⚡ Look at the photographs.

⚡ What things are the same about the animals?
What things are different?

⚡ What do animals need to stay alive and to grow?

PCM 1

⚡ Use Photocopy Master 1 to show your ideas.
Compare your ideas with the others in your group.

Animals have a life cycle. The life cycle includes birth, growth, reproduction and death.

All animals are born.
They feed and grow into adults.
When they are adults, they can make more animals like themselves.
This is called **reproduction**.
For most animals, a male animal and a female animal are needed for reproduction.
All animals grow older and eventually die.
This completes the life cycle.

Task 2 Spot the life cycle stages

 Look at the photographs.
They show the different stages of the life cycle.
Which photographs show:

- birth

- growth

- reproduction

- death?

 Now look at the pictures on Photocopy Master 2.
Cut out the pictures. Put them in the correct order.

Task 3 — What a baby needs

 Babies have special needs.
Look at a photograph of you as a baby.

 What did you need when you were a baby?
Draw and write to show your ideas.

 What did you eat?
Draw and write to show your ideas.

 Make a record of the different stages of
your life, like the one shown on the right.

My Personal Record Name..............		
	Weight	Height
at birth		
age 1		
age 5		
age 7		
age 10		

Task 4 — Keeping the life cycle going

 Look at the picture.
It shows how the life cycle
keeps going.

baby → child → teenager → adult → grandparent

 Make a zig-zag book of
the stages of your life cycle.

 Now copy and complete the table below.
Draw and write to show what the
different stages of your life might be like.

parents

baby → child → teenager → adult → grandparent

 Think about these things:

- What will you look like?

- What clothes will you wear?

- When might you have children?

- What important things will you have to
do as a parent?

- What will you be like when you have
grown old?

- Who might be able to help you when
you are old?

parents

baby

Me at:					
10	14	18	30	50	70

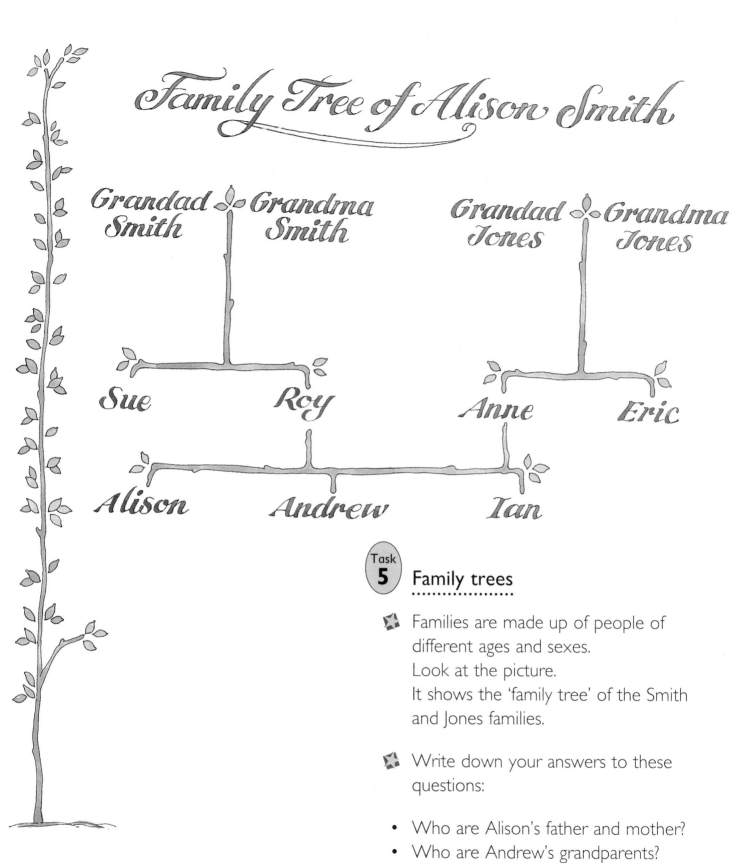

Family Tree of Alison Smith

Grandad Smith ⚭ Grandma Smith

Grandad Jones ⚭ Grandma Jones

Sue   Roy

Anne   Eric

Alison   Andrew   Ian

Task 5   **Family trees**

⬧ Families are made up of people of different ages and sexes.
Look at the picture.
It shows the 'family tree' of the Smith and Jones families.

⬧ Write down your answers to these questions:

- Who are Alison's father and mother?
- Who are Andrew's grandparents?
- Who are Anne's parents?
- What will happen to the life cycle of this family if Alison, Andrew and Ian do not have children?

⬧ Now make your own family tree or a pretend one.

⬧ What will happen to this family tree if no one has any children?

You will need:

- a set of counters, in two different colours
- a container for the counters
- a dice
- 4-6 people to play the game.

Task **6** The Survival Game

① Use the board on the opposite page or make your own board to play the Survival Game. Make some counters in two different colours. Make a boat-shaped container for the counters.

② Each player needs a container (the boat) and six counters in two colours. The counters are the people in your boat – three males and three females. Use different colours for the males and females.

③ Start at the bottom of the board and travel along the squares.

④ Throw a dice to see who starts.

⑤ Move along the board according to the score on the dice. The squares you land on show how many children are born or how many people die.

⑥ The winner is the boat that reaches the end with the most males and females on it. If you have all males or all females in the boat, you cannot win. In this game, you have to have a male and female to make more children to keep the life cycle going.

Task
7

Reproduce or die out!
....

To make a new animal, two special cells have to join together. One is usually an egg from the mother. The other is a sperm from the father. These are the **reproductive cells**.

✦ Write your answers to these questions. Use other books to help you.

① Can any part of the body be used to make a baby?

② What are the male and female reproductive cells called?

③ What has to happen to the reproductive cells if a new life is to be started?

④ For how long does a human baby have to grow before it is born?

⑤ When a baby has been born, what does the mother's body do so that she can feed it?

⑥ Who usually cares for the baby?

⑦ When the new baby has grown up, how could the life cycle keep going?

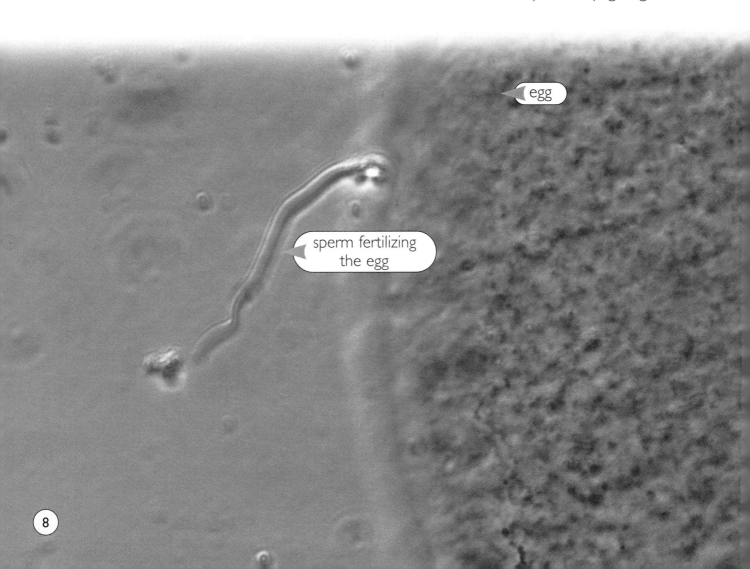

Read the newspaper story.

Daily Earth
23 May 2100

Scientists find the key to life!

Scientists have solved the mystery of why we grow old. They have developed a new drug which will help to keep body parts such as the heart and lungs working better. The drug will keep them healthy for longer. It means that we could now live for ever.

 Should we use the new drug to keep us alive for ever?
Make lists of the advantages and disadvantages of the new drug.
Put them in a table like this:

Advantages of using new life drug	Disadvantages of using new life drug

 Use your lists to write the rest of the newspaper story.

Fascinating life cycles

Some animals have special ways of reproducing.

The male three-spined stickleback builds a nest for the female to lay eggs in. The male fertilizes the eggs in the nest with the sperm. Then he guards the nest until the young fish are born. They hatch from the eggs. During this time, the male stickleback has a red chest. This is like a warning sign to other fish to keep away.

The seahorse is a fish. The male seahorse broods the eggs in its mouth. It cares for the young.

After a male and female spider have mated, the female eats the male. This stops the male mating with any other females.

Kangaroos give birth to very tiny babies. After they are born, they climb into a pouch on the mother's tummy. They suck milk made by the mother in special glands. These glands are called **mammary glands**.

Emperor penguins live in Antarctica. They lay their eggs on ice and do not make a nest. They lay one egg and hold it on their feet. In one place in Antarctica, about 300,000 pairs of emperor penguins nest side by side.

Bats, like us, are mammals. Female bats usually have one baby each year. They rarely have twins. This is because they would have to carry extra weight when they were pregnant. This would make flying difficult. To keep a good number of bats in the population they breed over many years. A bat's life span is about 20 years.

Animals	Life span (years)
chimpanzee	44
Chinese alligator	52
dog	20
eagle owl	68
Galapagos tortoise	100+
herring gull	41
horse	46
house mouse	3
human (Madame Jeanne Calment, France, 1997)	120+
Indian elephant	70
monkey	29
vampire bat	13

Life spans

A life span is the time between starting life at birth and ending it with death. Different animals have different life spans.
The table gives information about life spans of some animals.

✱ Make another table of this information. Put the animal with the longest life span at the top and the one with the shortest life span at the bottom.

PCM 3

Use Photocopy Master 3.

✱ Now make a bar graph of the information in your table.

✱ Answer these questions:

- Which animal has the longest life span?

- Which animal has the shortest life span?

- How much longer is a vampire bat likely to live than a house mouse?

- How much longer is an eagle owl likely to live than a herring gull?

- Why do you think some animals have longer life spans than others?

house mouse

Galapagos tortoise

⭐ Health can be affected by different things.

Just like a car, our body can be harmed if it is not cared for properly.

We can become ill if harmful things get into our body.

Harmful things can get into our body:

- when we breathe

- when we eat and drink

- through our skin.

Tobacco smoke, alcohol, dirty air and other gases and **ultra-violet** light are some things which can make us ill. You need to know about these things so that you can protect your body from harm.

What type of harmful things do these photographs show?

Task 10   Smoking and health

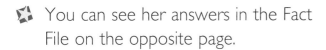

A health visitor came to Duncan's school. He asked her some questions about smoking.

✧ You can see her answers in the Fact File on the opposite page.

✧ Complete this table.

Read the Fact File to help you. Use Photocopy Master 4.

Material in smoke	What it is like	What it does to the body
		Stops some blood carrying oxygen
Nicotine		
	Black and sticky	

Fact File
Smoking

What is smoking?
It is when tobacco is burned to produce fumes of gas which can be breathed into our lungs. Some smoke breathed into the lungs will stay in our body.

What can be smoked?
Cigarettes, cigars, and pipe tobacco.

What is in smoke?
Mostly **carbon monoxide**, **nicotine** and **tar**.

What can these things do to us?
Carbon monoxide is poisonous. It stops blood carrying oxygen so that the heart and lungs have to work harder.

So what is nicotine?
Nicotine makes teeth and fingers yellow and smelly. It harms the heart, blood vessels and the nervous system. Nicotine makes people want to keep smoking. It makes the heart beat faster.

What makes smokers cough?
Tar, which is black and sticky. It coats the lungs, making it harder for oxygen to enter the blood.

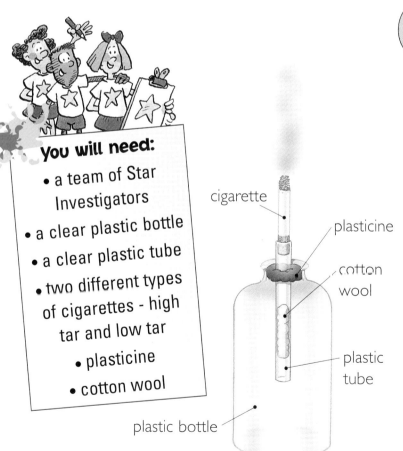

you will need:
- a team of Star Investigators
- a clear plastic bottle
- a clear plastic tube
- two different types of cigarettes - high tar and low tar
- plasticine
- cotton wool

cigarette

plasticine

cotton wool

plastic tube

plastic bottle

⚠ **Safety point: This activity must be done with your teacher, not on your own, and it must be done outdoors.**

Task 11

I n v e s t i g a t i o n
What is in cigarette smoke?

You can use a testing machine to find out how much tar different brands of cigarettes contain.

✷ With your teacher, make a testing machine like the one in the picture.

✷ Design a table for your results.

✷ Test for how long each type of cigarette burns. The tar will collect on the cotton wool.

✷ Write down the results in your table.

◆ Now try this

✷ Use the information from your test to make a poster or leaflet to persuade people not to smoke.

To smoke or not to smoke?

Do you think you will smoke when you grow up?

 PCM 5,6

✦ Use Photocopy Master 5 to write down some reasons for smoking and some reasons against.

✦ Count up the number of people in your class who say they will smoke and the number of people who say they will not smoke. Record the numbers on Photocopy Master 6.

✦ Now make a bar chart showing the information on Photocopy Master 6.

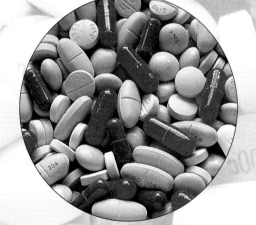

Fact File

Medicines

All medicines are drugs.
Medicines can help cure us when we are ill.
For some medicines, we have to go to the doctor.
Some can be bought from a chemist or supermarket.
Some drugs are harmful.
Some drugs are **illegal** (it is against the law to use them).

Everyday drugs

 Look at the pictures.
Some everyday things such as coffee, tea and cola contain caffeine.
Caffeine is a **stimulant** drug.
It makes the heart beat faster and people feel less sleepy.
Nicotine is also a drug. It is also a stimulant like caffeine.
Alcohol is a drug. Alcohol can affect people in different ways.

These are some of the ways that alcohol can affect people:

- it can make them argue

- it can make them do things more slowly

- it makes them unsafe to drive a car.

 Copy and complete this table.

Everyday product	Drug it contains	How it is taken	How it affects our bodies and behaviour
Wine	Alcohol		
Coffee			
Tea	Caffeine		
Beer			
Cigarette	Nicotine		

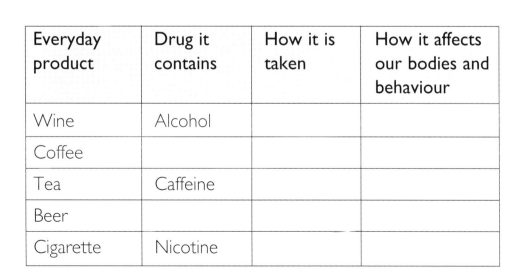

Investigation

How does cola change the heart rate of a water flea?

Water fleas are small animals living in fresh water.
They have a small heart.
This can be seen under a microscope.

In an investigation, some scientists observed a water flea in water and then cola.
They did the investigation to show the effect that water and cola had on the heartbeat of the flea.

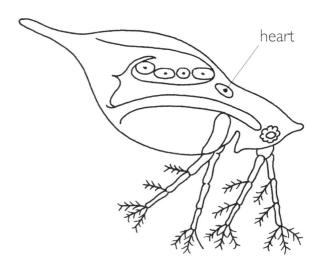

heart

The scientists counted the number of beats in a minute. They did this three times for water and three times for cola.
The results are shown in the table.

Liquid	Number of beats per minute				
	1st go	2nd go	3rd go	Total	Average
Water	75	84	70		
Cola	110	115	125		

 Write down your answers to these questions.

- What is the total number of heartbeats in water in 3 minutes?

- What is the total number of heartbeats in cola in 3 minutes?

- What is the average number of heartbeats in water and cola?

- How much faster was the average heartbeat in cola than water?

- Why do you think it beats faster in cola?

Water flea

Fact File

Sunbathing

The Sun helps us to make vitamin D in our skin, which is good for us.
But too much sunbathing can harm us.
Changes happen in the skin if we have too much sun.
This can cause a disease called skin cancer.

Task 15 Safe sunbathing

PCM 7-9

☀ Read the play on Photocopy Masters 7 and 8. At the end of each act, stop and fill in the correct part of the Fact Sheet on Photocopy Master 9.

◆ **Now try this**

Task 16 Safe sun care

☀ Choose **one** of the following:

① Design a leaflet or make a poster on safe sunbathing.
Use the information on your Fact Sheet.

or

② Make up a rhyme about being in hot and sunny weather.

☀ Then present your work to the rest of the class.
Which was the best way of giving the message about safe sunbathing?
How do you know?

Fact File

Asthma

One in every ten children has asthma.

During an attack, a person with asthma becomes breathless. He or she wheezes and coughs.
His or her chest feels tight. The air tubes in the lungs narrow. Breathing is then harder.

These are some of the things that scientists think can cause asthma:

- the house dust-mite

- air pollution

- foam mattresses.

house dust-mite

Why is this cyclist wearing a mask?

Task 17 Measuring breath

A peak flow meter can be used to measure how well someone with asthma can breathe out.

 Look at the information on Photocopy Master 10.
Make a graph or table to show the readings.

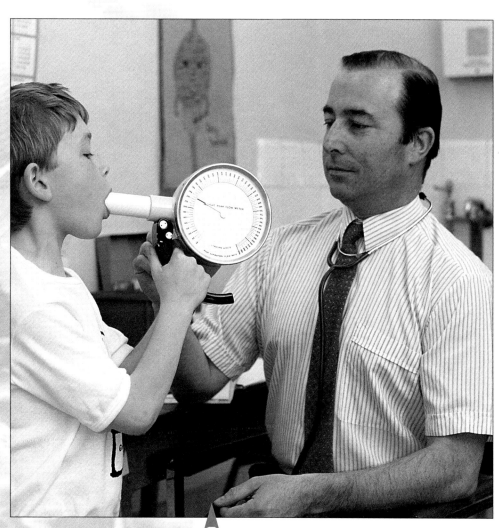

Using a peak flow meter.

Animals have body systems.

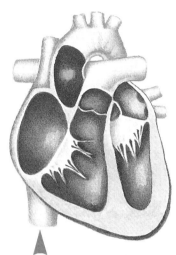

heart, part of
circulatory system

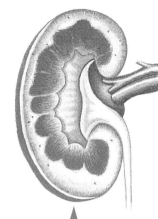

kidney, part of
excretory system

brain, part of
nervous system

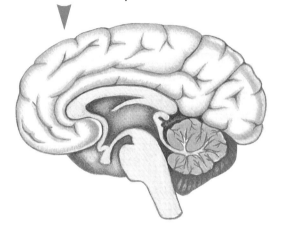

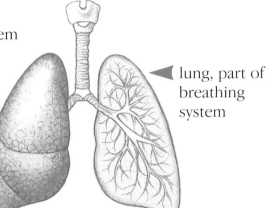

lung, part of
breathing
system

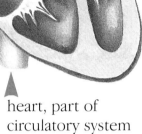

stomach, part of
digestive system ▶

Fact File

Body Systems

Our bodies are made up of special
body systems.
There are different body systems
to do different jobs.

These are our main body systems:

- the **breathing** system
- the **circulatory** system
- the **digestive** system
- the **excretory** system
- the **nervous** system
- the **reproductive** system
- the **skeletal** system.

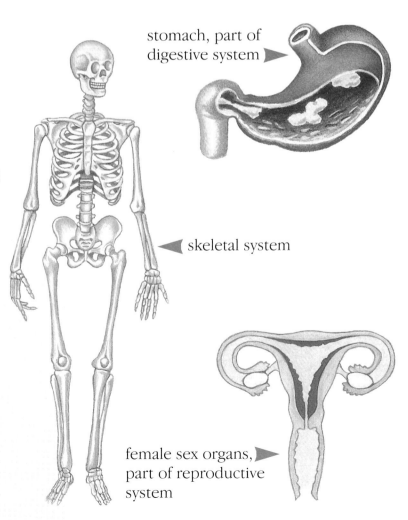

◀ skeletal system

female sex organs, ▶
part of reproductive
system

You will need:
- a board
- Photocopy Masters 11-13
- dice
- a shaker
- 4-6 players

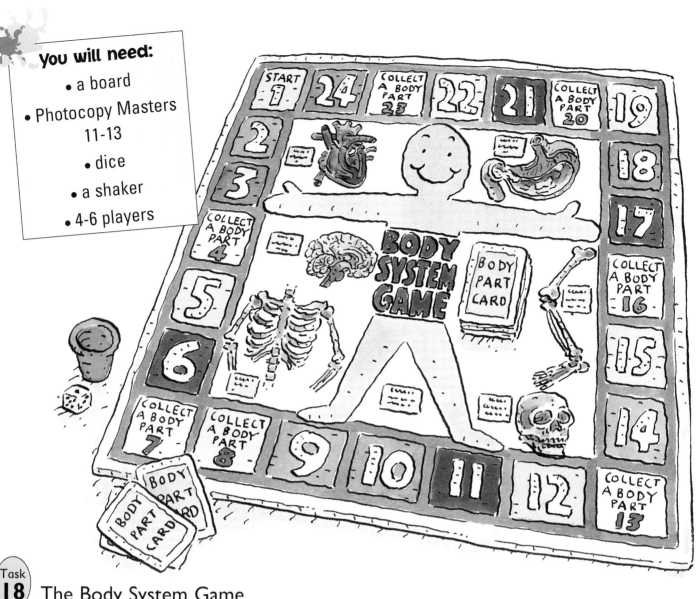

Task 18 The Body System Game

 Make a board for the game. Use the pictures to give you some ideas.

PCM 11-13

 Make some cards of different body parts. Use Photocopy Masters 11-13.

How to play

① Shuffle the cards and place them, face down, in the centre of the board.

② The person who throws the dice with the highest number starts.

③ Take it in turns to move around the board.

④ When you land on a 'body part' square, take a card from the centre of the board.

⑤ You can choose to swap cards instead of throwing the dice when it is your turn.

⑥ Keep going around until you have collected a complete body system.

⑦ When all the cards have been collected, take it in turns to swap cards so that each person can make complete systems.

 Do you have enough systems to live?

 If not, what do you need? Why?

Task **19** Body System Quiz

⬧ After you have played the Body System game, answer these questions.

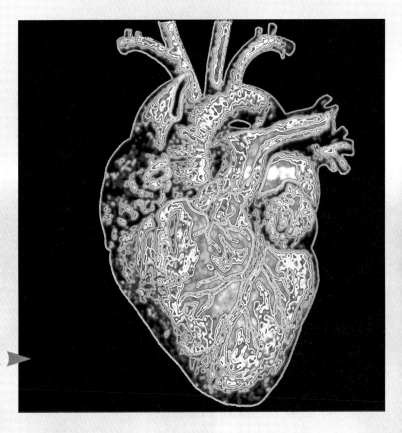

① Blood is pumped around our bodies. ▶
   What pumps the blood?
   What system does it belong to?

② The digestive system changes food so that it can pass through the gut into the blood. Why does it need to do this? What are the different parts of the digestive system?

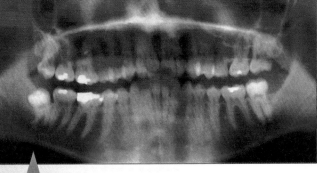

③ Teeth start the process of digestion. How do teeth help digestion?

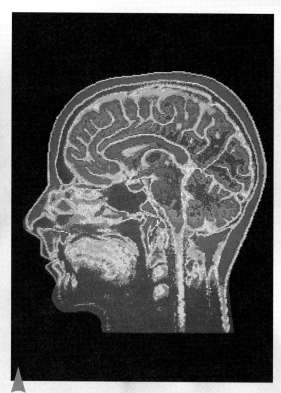

④ The brain controls all the life processes in the body.
Which system does it belong to?

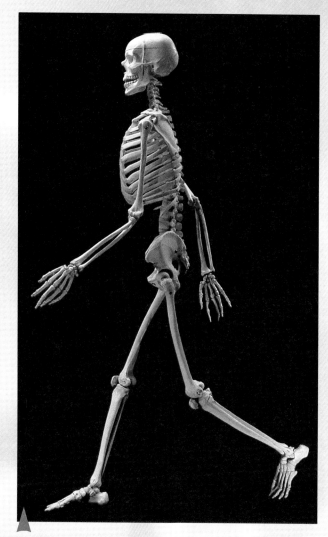

⑤ The skeletal system is made of bones and muscles.
What does it do? How do muscles move bones?

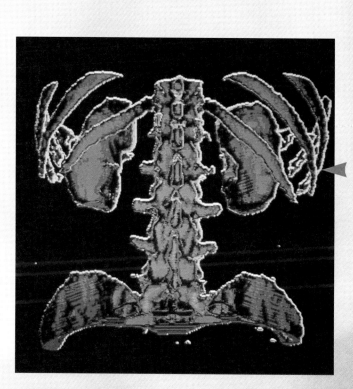

⑥ Kidneys remove poisonous waste from the blood.
Which system do the kidneys belong to?

Body Repair Gang

Unhealthy Henry has some problems with his body!

 Look at the pictures on the opposite page. Henry has sent Class 5 some e-mails, describing how he is feeling.

 Read each e-mail. Decide which body system is involved.

 Send messages to Henry to help him.

PCM
14,15

Use Photocopy Masters 14 and 15.

From:	Class 5
To:	Unhealthy Henry
Subject:	Help for your symptoms
Date:	05-27
Symptom:	Feeling sick because of over eating and drinking.
Advice:	Sip water. No food for 4 hours, then only eat light snacks.

I have been to a party and eaten and drunk too much. I have sickness and diarrhoea.

I have twisted my ankle. It is very swollen.

I have an abscess under my tooth, and it hurts.

I have a fever. I feel hot and I keep shivering. My body is covered in a rash.

The heart

- The heart pumps blood around the body and to the lungs.

- The heart is in the chest. It is protected by the ribs.

- The heart has four **chambers** – a right and left **atrium** and a right and left **ventricle**.

- The heart is about the size of a clenched fist.

- The right-hand side of the heart is separate from the left-hand side.

- The right-hand side receives blood from the body with carbon dioxide and then pumps it to the lungs.

- The left-hand side of the heart receives blood that has travelled from the lungs with oxygen. It then pumps blood around the body.

- Blood leaves the heart in arteries.

- Blood returns to the heart in veins.

- Each beat of the left ventricle of the heart can be felt as a pulse where an artery passes over a bone.

- The heart beats about 70 times a minute when resting.

- When resting, it takes 6 seconds for blood to be pumped to the brain and back to the heart.

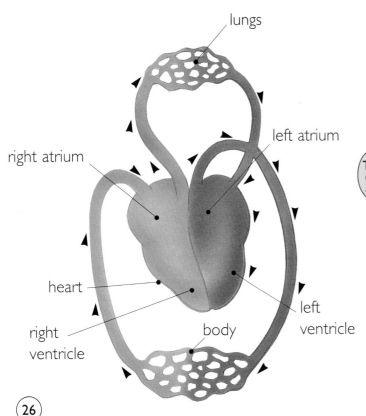

lungs

right atrium

left atrium

heart

right ventricle

body

left ventricle

◆ Now try this

Task 21 Information on the heart

 How can you help your friends understand where the heart is and what it does?
Think of some different ways that the information in the Fact File could be used to help your friends understand how the heart works.

 Try these out on your friends.

You will need:

- some red and blue counters (at least 42)
- bean bags
- game, drawn on the playground.

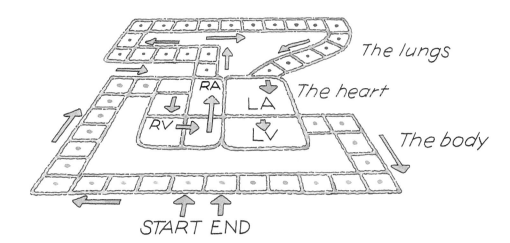

The lungs

The heart

The body

RA

LA

RV

LV

START END

Heart Hopscotch!

This is a game to help you understand how the heart pumps blood around the body.
The heart pumps blood to all parts of the body.

Every living part of the body makes carbon dioxide which must be breathed out of the lungs into the air if we are to stay alive.
In this game, you are the blood carrying oxygen and carbon dioxide.

How to play heart hopscotch in the playground:

Use blue counters for carbon dioxide.
Use red counters for oxygen.

① Ask your teacher to draw a large heart and lungs on the playground surface like the one in the picture.

② Put a blue counter in all the body squares.
These stand for harmful carbon dioxide made by the body.

③ Put red counters in the squares of the lungs.
These stand for vital oxygen.

④ Take five red counters and go to the start square.

⑤ Throw a bean bag into a square then hop to the bean bag square.

⑥ Put down a red counter outside the square you land on and pick up the blue one. You are swapping oxygen for carbon dioxide.

⑦ Throw the bean bag again and continue to 'circulate' by hopping towards the heart and lungs. In the lungs leave blue (carbon dioxide) counters and pick up red ones from the squares you land on.

⑧ Hop back to the heart and into the 'body'.

⑨ Take it in turns to circulate round the body. Follow each other round.
The next person starts when the hopper reaches the heart.
Hopping exercises the heart as well as the body. Count your pulse rate before and after hopping.
When is it fastest? Why?

⑩ Some of your group should replace the blue counters in the 'body' squares and red ones in the 'lung' squares as you go around the system.

Fact File — Animal hearts

Not all animals have a heart, but many do. Their hearts are not all like our hearts, but they do the same job.
The job of a heart is to pump fluid, usually blood, around the body.

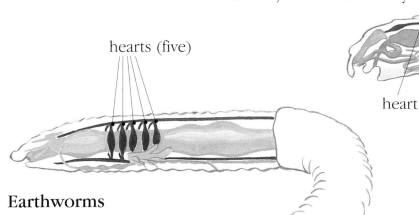

heart

hearts (five)

Earthworms

An earthworm has five small circular hearts.
These are weak pumps.
They pump blood from the blood vessel you can see on its back to the one on its 'tummy'.

Insects

An insect has a heart which is like a long tube passing through its body from the abdomen to the head.
Blood flows only from the abdomen (tail) of the insect to its head. It then drips out to bathe the other body parts.
It has valves which only allow blood to move from 'tail' to head.

heart

Frogs

A frog has a small heart with three **chambers**. Two of the chambers receive blood from its lungs and its body. One chamber pumps blood with and without oxygen either to the lungs or around the body. A frog's heart is quite weak, but it can pump blood all around the body.

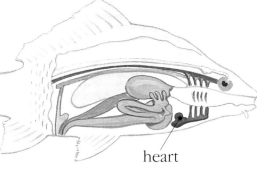

heart

Fish

A fish has an s-shaped heart. It has two main **chambers**. The heart pumps blood to the gills and then it goes all around the body before returning to the heart.

Birds

A bird has a heart with four chambers (two **pumping ventricles** and two **receiving chambers**) just like a mammal.

Blood is pumped from the right ventricle to the lungs to get oxygen and get rid of carbon dioxide.

Blood with oxygen returns to the left atrium and is squeezed into the ventricle below.

Like the human heart, it is the left ventricle that pumps blood with oxygen around the body.

Birds' hearts beat faster than ours. The number of beats varies for different types of birds.

heart

North American humming bird ▶

robin ▶

sparrow

crow

Bird	Number of beats per minute
North American humming bird	1000
robin	570
sparrow	570
crow	342

- Can you think of some reasons why birds' hearts beat so fast?

- How does the size of the bird affect the number of its heartbeats per minute?

Task 23 Let's get to the heart of the matter

⚡ Draw and write to show what you think makes a healthy heart.

⚡ Class 5 did a survey to find out who they thought was fit. There were 15 boys and 15 girls in the class. They were asked to name:

- three fit people in the class
- three fit adults
- three fit international athletes.

The table shows their answers.

Questions	Number of answers naming boys and men	Number of answers naming girls and women
① Name 3 fit people in the class	60	30
② Name 3 fit adults	66	24
③ Name 3 international sports people	75	15

⚡ Answer these questions:

① How many answers given by Class 5 referred to males?

② How many female international athletes were named by the class? How many male international athletes were named by the class?

③ Why do you think there were more answers naming boys and men than girls and women?

 Task 24 Fitness profile

Look at Helen's Fitness Profile.
Answer these questions:

① What do you think Helen did to collect this data?

② How could you find out how long it took for her pulse to return to normal?

Helen's Fitness Profile	pulse rate (beats per minute)	breathing rate (per minute)
When resting before exercise	64	10
Straight after vigorous exercise	180	30
1 minute after exercise	160	30
2 minutes after exercise	140	26
3 minutes after exercise	120	22
4 minutes after exercise	114	18
5 minutes after exercise	96	16
6 minutes after exercise	70	12

Fitness Plan

Type of exercise	Continuous activity using the legs, for example, roller skating, swimming, football, martial arts, mountain biking, or cycling, walking the dog
How often?	3-5 times per week
How long?	12-20 minutes each session
How hard?	In the gym: high intensity work for 3-5 minutes, followed by lower intensity work for 3-5 minutes

⚠️ Check with your teacher first before trying this activity.

◆ Now try this

Make your own Fitness Profile like Helen's. Answer these questions:

① How long did it take for your pulse to return to normal?

② Is your pulse rate faster or slower than Helen's at rest?

③ How long did it take for your breathing rate to return to normal?

④ Do you think you are fit? Why?

⑤ Design a leaflet or poster to show young people how to keep fit.

Use the Fitness Plan on the left for ideas.

Checkpoint

birth

can give

mother and father

look after a

baby

Task 25 Concept map

 Make a concept map like this.
Use these words: reproduce, birth, baby, grow, mother, father, care, grow old, die.

Task 26 Body systems

Make a list of the most important body systems.

Draw and write to show what each system does.

Make a table. Use Photocopy Master 16.

Body system	What it does
Skeletal system	
	Gets rid of waste

Task 27 Keeping healthy

What can you do to keep healthy?

Draw a picture of yourself.

Label the heart and lungs.

List ways in which you can keep these body parts healthy.

32